Profiles of the Presidents

JOHN
TYLER

★ ★ ★

Profiles of the Presidents

JOHN TYLER

by Robin S. Doak

Content Adviser: Harry Rubenstein, Curator of Political History Collections, National Museum of American History, Smithsonian Institution

Reading Adviser: Dr. Linda D. Labbo, Department of Reading Education, College of Education, The University of Georgia

COMPASS POINT BOOKS ✦ MINNEAPOLIS, MINNESOTA

Compass Point Books
3109 West 50th Street, #115
Minneapolis, MN 55410

Visit Compass Point Books on the Internet at *www.compasspointbooks.com*
or e-mail your request to *custserv@compasspointbooks.com*

Photographs ©: White House Collection, Courtesy White House Historical Association, cover, 1, 32, 40; Hulton/Archive by Getty Images, 7, 8, 18, 24, 31, 35, 37, 38, 42, 43 (top), 45, 46, 47, 54 (all), 55 (right), 56 (top right), 57 (top right), 58 (all), 59 (bottom right); North Wind Picture Archives, 9 (top), 10, 16, 39, 48, 49, 55 (left), 59 (left); Bettmann/Corbis, 9 (bottom), 11, 19, 26, 27, 35; Corbis, 12; Lombard Antiquarian Maps & Prints, 13, 25, 56 (left); *The House of Representatives* by Samuel Finley Morse, 1822, oil on canvas, in the Collection of the Corcoran Gallery of Art, Museum Purchase, Gallery Fund (#11.14), 14; Giraudon/Art Resource, N.Y., 15; Michael Maslan Historic Photographs/Corbis, 17; National Portrait Gallery, Smithsonian Institution/Art Resource, N.Y., 20; Stapleton Collection/Corbis, 21; Library of Congress, 22, 29, 59 (top right); Stock Montage, 23, 33, 57 (left); U.S. Naval Historical Center, 30; David J. & Janice L. Frent Collection/Corbis, 41; Dave G. Houser/Corbis, 44; James P. Rowan, 50; Department of Rare Books and Special Collections, University of Rochester Library, 56 (bottom right); Texas Library & Archives Commission, 57 (middle right); Bruce Burkhardt/Corbis, 57 (bottom right).

Editors: E. Russell Primm, Emily J. Dolbear, Melissa McDaniel, and Catherine Neitge
Photo Researcher: Svetlana Zhurkina
Photo Selector: Linda S. Koutris
Designer: The Design Lab
Cartographer: XNR Productions, Inc.

Library of Congress Cataloging-in-Publication Data
Doak, Robin S. (Robin Santos), 1963–
  John Tyler / by Robin S. Doak.
    p. cm.— (Profiles of the presidents)
Includes bibliographical references (p.) and index.
Contents: The accidental president—Early life—A rising star—Road to the White House—A rocky presidency—Working for the South—Later life—Glossary—John Tyler's life at a glance—John Tyler's life and times—World events—Understanding John Tyler and his presidency.
  ISBN 0-7565-0258-6 (hardcover)
 1. Tyler, John, 1790–1862—Juvenile literature. 2. Presidents—United States—Biography—Juvenile literature. [1. Tyler, John, 1790–1862. 2. Presidents.] I. Title. II. Series.
  E397 .D63 2003   2002010001

Table of Contents

★ ★ ★

NOTE: In this book, words that are defined in the glossary are in **bold** *the first time they appear in the text.*

The Accidental President

★ ★ ★

No one ever expected John Tyler to become president of the United States. When Tyler ran for vice president in 1840, even his own political party didn't care much about his views. When President William Henry Harrison died unexpectedly in 1841, however, Tyler took control. No president had ever died in office before Harrison. By acting quickly and firmly, Tyler set the standard for an orderly transfer of power.

As president, Tyler soon showed that he intended to do things his way. He was determined and unwilling to give an inch. He would remain true to his own principles, no matter what his own party or the public thought. As a result, he had a troubled term in office. Tyler was always at odds with Congress. He was even thrown out of his own political party. Some people even wanted to throw him out of office!

Tyler owned a **plantation** in Virginia. A slave owner, Tyler wanted to keep the government's power in the hands of the wealthy. He was also a stubborn supporter of **states' rights.** He didn't want the federal government to be any stronger than it already was. Throughout his career, Tyler did his best to defeat laws that gave power to the federal government.

Tyler always tried to stand firm and be constant. He failed, however, to realize that he lived in a world that was rapidly changing. Slavery, which Tyler himself practiced and defended, was beginning to tear the nation apart.

▼ *President John Tyler stood firmly by his principles.*

Early Life

★ ★ ★

John Tyler was born on March 29, 1790, at Greenway Estate in Charles City County, Virginia. John's family was wealthy and well respected. His father, John Tyler Sr., owned a 1,200-acre (4,856-hectare) tobacco plantation with forty slaves. John Sr. had fought in the Revolutionary

Tyler was born in ▶ this house in Charles City County, Virginia.

War (1775–1783) and was a friend of Thomas Jefferson's. He served the state of Virginia as a governor and a judge. John's mother, Mary Armistead, died when John Jr. was just seven years old.

John was very close to his father. As a boy, he listened to his father talk about politics and government. John's father believed that each state should have the power to make its own laws. As a slaveholder, John Sr. also believed that slavery should be allowed in the Southern states.

▲ Thomas Jefferson

◀ Tyler's father owned slaves and believed that other Southerners should be allowed to do the same.

As little John grew older, he adopted many of his father's beliefs and views.

John had two brothers and five sisters. They were lucky to grow up in a wealthy Virginia family. John learned how to ride a horse, manage a farm, and play the violin. John was a serious and sometimes moody child. He was also quite stubborn, a trait that would stay with him throughout his life.

John was a good student. When he was twelve years old, he was sent away to the grammar school at William and Mary College in nearby Williamsburg, Virginia. He began college there three years later.

Tyler attented ▼ William and Mary College.

◄ *John Tyler as a Virginia attorney*

At college, John was interested in law and politics. After he graduated in 1807, he returned to Greenway Estate and began studying to be a lawyer.

After two years of study, Tyler was allowed to practice law in Virginia. A tall, slim young man who carried himself proudly, Tyler cut a dashing figure in court. He quickly made a name for himself. He became known as an ambitious, forceful, and honest young lawyer. Above all, he was famous for his powerful courtroom speeches.

In 1811, Tyler was appointed to Virginia's House of Delegates, the state's lawmaking body. Sadness soon followed this success, however, when John Sr. died. Tyler's father left his son 500 acres (202 hectares) of land and a number of slaves. Now wealthy in his own right, Tyler decided that the time had come to start a family. On his twenty-third birthday, he married Letitia Christian.

The capitol in ▼
Richmond, Virginia

◄ *Letitia Christian Tyler*

Letitia, like John, came from a wealthy Virginia family. She was a beautiful and refined young woman. Over the years, John and Letitia had eight children together, although one, Anne, died when she was a baby. Throughout her marriage, Letitia devoted herself to her husband and family. Even after she was partly **paralyzed** by a **stroke** in 1839, Letitia continued to cook and oversee the family's affairs.

A Rising Star

★ ★ ★

As a young lawyer and politician, John Tyler was well known and well liked in his home state. In 1817, Virginia sent Tyler to the U.S. House of Representatives. The young man quickly made his views and beliefs clear. Like his father, Tyler firmly supported states' rights. He let it be known that he would work to stop any politician who was trying to make the federal government more powerful.

John Tyler represented Virginia in the House of Representatives.

Tyler also believed that lawmakers should carefully obey the U.S. **Constitution**. Tyler believed that the Constitution clearly spells out the federal government's responsibilities. During his long career, he tried to remain faithful to his understanding of the Constitution—even when it put him at odds with other politicians. This faithfulness would cause some people to dislike Tyler.

◄ Tyler believed in the absolute authority of the U.S. Constitution. This eighteenth-century engraving is from the *Bibliothèque nationale* of France.

Tyler supported slavery.

Representative Tyler also spoke out on behalf of the interests and legal rights of slave owners. The issue of slavery was dividing the nation. Over the years, Tyler's views in favor of slavery would bring him into conflict with politicians from the North. Many Northerners wanted to end slavery.

Tyler remained true to his father's ideals. These were the beliefs the younger Tyler had grown up with. Times were changing, however. The United States was growing by leaps and bounds. Industry was becoming more important to the nation's economy. More men across the nation were gaining the right to vote. The United States was beginning to move toward a true government "by the people."

Tyler quickly became frustrated as a U.S. representative. In 1821, he left Congress and returned home to his family.

Tyler was ambitious, though. He would not sit idle for long. In 1825, he became governor of Virginia. Two years later, Tyler returned to Washington, D.C., this time as a senator. Senator Tyler became a member of the Democratic Party. Founded in 1828, the Democratic Party was made up of politicians who were against a strong central government.

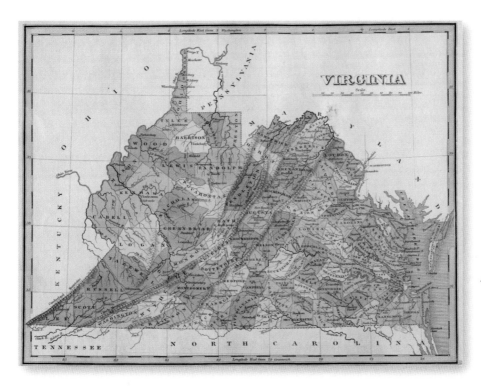

◀ *Tyler served as governor of Virginia.*

In the Senate, Tyler supported bills that he thought protected states' rights. As he had in the House, he spoke out loudly against those bills he believed gave the federal government too much power. For example, Tyler voted against spending federal money on state projects. He also opposed having a national bank with state branches.

Tyler was a strong supporter of states' rights, but he didn't think that states should be allowed to pick and choose which federal laws they wanted to follow. So in 1832, Tyler opposed South Carolina's attempt to try to nullify, or ignore, some federal laws and taxes. He thought that South Carolina had gone too far.

Democratic ▼ president Andrew Jackson

During Tyler's eight years as a U.S. senator, he came to dislike Democratic president Andrew Jackson. Tyler had once supported the popular president, but he became convinced that Jackson was too power-hungry. Tyler joined the growing group of politicians who disapproved of "King Andrew."

In 1834, Tyler voted to censure, or officially criticize, the president for one of his actions. Two years later, Virginia Democrats ordered Tyler to vote to remove the censure. He refused. Democrats were furious. They began calling him "**Turncoat** Tyler."

◄ *This political cartoon makes fun of what Tyler and others saw as Andrew Jackson's growing ambition. It shows Jackson in the robes and crown of a king trampling on the Constitution.*

Tyler left the Senate in 1836. He also left the Democratic Party. He then joined the Whig Party. The Whigs were a new political party, formed in 1834 to oppose President Jackson.

Road to the White House

★ ★ ★

In 1836, the Whigs hoped to take control of the White House. They came up with an unusual plan. Instead of choosing one person to run against Democrat Martin Van Buren, the Whigs chose three. They thought that they could defeat Van Buren by having different people run in areas where each one was popular. If nobody won more than 50 percent of the votes, the election would be decided in the House of Representatives.

Martin Van Buren ▾

The Whigs chose Daniel Webster from Massachusetts to run in the Northeast. William Henry Harrison from Ohio ran in the West. Hugh L. White from Tennessee ran in the South. The Whigs asked John Tyler to run as vice president with both Harrison and White.

The Whig plan did not work. All three Whigs were beaten in the election. The Whigs, however, learned from their mistakes. Four years later, they were ready to try again. This time, the Whigs chose just one person, William Henry Harrison, to run against President Martin Van Buren.

▲ Daniel Webster

Like Tyler, Harrison had been born in Virginia. The old army veteran had spent most of his life in the West. There he had bought land and fought Native Americans.

William Henry Harrison led the charge at the Battle of Tippecanoe against Tecumseh and his Native American forces.

Harrison was known throughout the nation as "Old Tippecanoe," for a battle he had won in 1811.

Old Tippecanoe was popular with voters in the West. Now, all the Whigs needed was someone who would attract votes in the South. Once again, Whig leaders turned to John Tyler.

If the Whigs had cared more about Tyler's beliefs, they might have chosen a different Southerner. Tyler had joined the Whigs to oppose Andrew Jackson, but he disagreed with many of the party's main ideas. The Whigs never asked him about his views, though.

The election of 1840 was very unusual. The Whigs told Harrison to avoid talking about the issues of the day. He was told to take no stands when speaking in public. The Whigs urged Tyler to stay home and not speak at all. He was happy to obey. Although he was a brilliant speaker in court and in Congress, Tyler disliked speaking in front of the common people. He spent most of the election **campaign** sitting on his front porch, managing his plantation, and playing with his children.

▼ *A parade for Harrison and running mate Tyler*

During the election, a Democratic newspaperman said that Old Tippecanoe would be happy to live out his days in a log cabin drinking **hard cider.** The Democrats thought that this statement would hurt Harrison's campaign. Instead, the Whigs used it to their advantage. They passed out hard cider at some events. They whipped the public into a frenzy. They held parades, bonfires, and rallies to win support for Harrison and Tyler. They

A campaign print showing Harrison (left) and a wounded Tippecanoe veteran

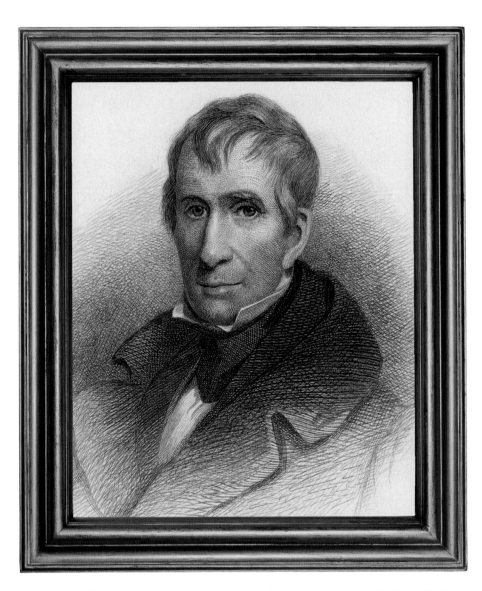

◀ *William Henry Harrison*

portrayed Harrison as a man of the people, and the Whig Party as the party for the average citizen.

The "Log Cabin and Hard Cider" campaign was fun. It appealed to voters. The Whigs used the **slogan**

"Tippecanoe and Tyler too." It was catchy, easy to remember, and often repeated. It was not a surprise, then, when William Henry Harrison easily defeated Martin Van Buren. Harrison would be the nation's ninth president.

On March 4, 1841, Harrison and Tyler both took the oath of office. It was a bitterly cold day. That didn't stop President Harrison from basking in his moment of

Harrison's ▶
inauguration

glory. Without a coat or a hat, Harrison braved the weather to deliver a rambling speech that lasted two hours. In the speech, Harrison promised to let Congress run the government. By the time he returned to the White House, Harrison was tired and not feeling well.

After being sworn in as vice president, Tyler went home to Virginia. For the next four weeks, his life went on as before. As the sun rose on April 5, 1841, however, Tyler was awakened by someone pounding on his door. It was a messenger from Washington with some urgent news: President Harrison was dead! The cold he had

▼ President Harrison died of pneumonia one month after taking office.

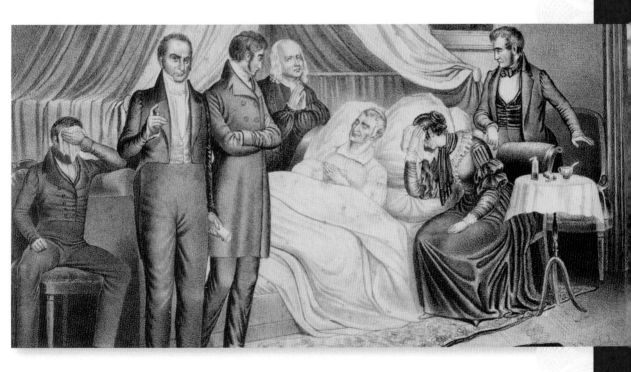

caught a month earlier had developed into pneumonia, a lung disease. President Harrison had died the day before. Tyler ate his breakfast, packed his clothes, and set off for Washington.

Tyler arrived in Washington on April 6 to find the capital in an uproar. No president had ever died in office before. The Constitution was not clear about how much power the vice president should get in this situation. People began to wonder what Tyler would do next. Would he take the oath of office and become the nation's next president? Would he accept the title of "acting president" and call for a new presidential election? Would he step down and allow Congress to select a new president?

People didn't have to wait long for Tyler's next move. The same day he arrived in the capital, Tyler had himself sworn in as the tenth president of the United States. He declared that he would serve out the rest of Harrison's four-year term.

Tyler's quick, firm response set an example for what future vice presidents would do when presidents died. Tyler's actions, however, caused an uproar in Congress. Politicians—Whigs and Democrats alike—were furious. Many demanded that Tyler step down. When he refused,

◄ Tyler was in
Virginia when he
received news of
Harrison's death.

people began calling him "His Accidency." They sent mail
addressed to the "Acting President" or the "Vice President–
Acting President." Tyler returned all such mail unopened.

George E. Badger served as secretary of the navy under both Harrison and Tyler.

The Whigs were sure they could control Tyler and the government. Tyler had allowed all of Harrison's **cabinet** to keep their jobs. The first time the cabinet met with Tyler, they told him that President Harrison had let them make all the decisions. The cabinet was shocked by Tyler's response. "I shall be pleased to avail myself of your counsel and advice," Tyler said. "But I can never consent to being dictated to as to what I shall or shall not do." This was just the beginning of the power struggle between Tyler and the Whigs.

At War with Congress

★　★　★

Problems between John Tyler and the Whigs quickly went from bad to worse. In August 1841, Congress sent a bill to the White House for Tyler's approval. The bill,

▼ *Whig politician Henry Clay*

written by Whig leaders, created a national bank and raised taxes. Tyler **vetoed** the bill. He said that the bill threatened states' rights.

Politicians and the public went wild with anger when they heard about the veto. Powerful Whig senator Henry Clay demanded that Tyler leave the presidency at once. At night, angry mobs armed with rocks and guns marched to the White House. The drunken group woke up everyone in the White House. They terrified Tyler's sick wife and his children.

Inside the White House, Tyler and his servants took up weapons and waited for the people outside to calm down. The crowd shouted and threw rocks. Then they burned an **effigy** of the president on the White House lawn. Finally, they turned around and went home.

The White House during the 1840s ▶

If the angry mob thought they could scare Tyler into obeying Congress, they were wrong. Less than a month later, Congress sent Tyler a second bill to create a national bank. Again, Tyler vetoed the bill. During his time in office, the president would veto six bills sent to him by Congress.

The public reaction to Tyler's second veto was even stronger. People around the nation burned Tyler effigies. Hundreds of angry letters streamed into the White House. Many contained death threats.

▼ *Daniel Webster was the only member of Tyler's cabinet who did not quit.*

The Whigs were furious with Tyler. They decided that "Old Veto" must be punished. Shortly after the second veto, all but one member of Tyler's cabinet quit. The president quickly filled his cabinet with friends and allies from the Democratic Party.

The Whigs weren't finished with Tyler yet. On September 15, they got together and threw the president out of the Whig Party. They merrily announced in newspapers across the nation that Tyler was "a president without a party."

Tyler stood alone. He had no party to support him. The Democratic Party didn't want Tyler back. Democrats still remembered the president as "Turncoat Tyler," the man who had left their party to join the Whigs. Once again, the Whigs demanded that Tyler step down and allow them to choose a new president.

For the rest of Tyler's term, he and Congress were at war. Tyler's chief enemy was Senator Clay. In 1842, Clay began urging his fellow Whigs to **impeach** the president. Clay wanted the House of Representatives to accuse Tyler of high crimes in office. If he was then convicted by the Senate, he would be thrown out of office. On July 10, a **resolution** to start the impeachment was read in Congress. This was the first time such an action had ever been taken.

Tyler was enraged when he learned of the resolution. In a letter to a friend, Tyler wrote that the only thing he was guilty of was "the high crime of daring to have an opinion of my own. . . . I am abused in Congress and out, as man never was before—assailed as a traitor and threatened with impeachment. But let it pass." In January 1843, the impeachment effort was voted down.

While he was under threat of impeachment, Tyler and his family suffered a terrible tragedy. On September 10, 1842, Tyler's wife, Letitia, died quietly in the White House. Letitia had never fully recovered from her stroke in 1839. As first lady, Letitia had made just one public appearance, at the wedding of her daughter Elizabeth in January 1842. At other White House events, Tyler's daughter Letitia or his daughter-in-law Priscilla helped out.

Everyone who knew Letitia was saddened by her death. Tyler himself was filled with sorrow. For months, the White House was draped with black to mark the passing of the first lady.

▲ *Henry Clay wanted to impeach the president.*

Success and Happiness

★ ★ ★

Tyler's chief goal as president was to annex, or add, Texas to the nation. Texas had broken away from Mexico in 1836. Many Texans were now eager to become part of the United States. Many politicians, especially those in the North, did not want to annex Texas. The United States

*Texans celebrating ▶
their independence
from Mexico*

was equally divided between states that allowed slavery and those that did not. Texas allowed slavery, and Northern politicians did not want to add another slave state to the Union. When Tyler asked Congress to annex Texas, it refused.

Despite his many problems with Congress, John Tyler did have some successes as president. In 1841, Tyler signed the so-called Log Cabin Bill. The Log Cabin Bill allowed settlers to claim 160 acres (65 hectares) of land before it was offered publicly for sale. The bill boosted settlement in Iowa, Minnesota, Wisconsin, and Illinois. Tyler also encouraged settlement in the Oregon Territory.

▼ *The Log Cabin Bill increased settlement in frontier areas.*

Tyler ended the Seminole War (1835–1842). It had been a costly war between the United States and the Seminole Indians of Florida. The United States had spent millions of dollars fighting the war when the Seminole refused to give up their lands.

Osceola, a Seminole chief who led his people during the Seminole Wars

Tyler was most successful with foreign matters. In 1841, the United States began trading with China for the first time ever. Tyler also warned Great Britain and France to stay away from Hawaii. By doing this, he set the stage for Hawaii to one day become a U.S. state. Finally, Tyler's secretary of state, Daniel Webster, settled a long-running border dispute between Maine and Canada.

In December 1842, Tyler's personal life took a turn for the better. Three months after Letitia's death, Tyler met the woman who would become his second wife. Before Christmas, Julia Gardiner, the twenty-two-year-old daughter of New York senator David Gardiner, visited the White House with her family. Tyler was struck by the young woman's beauty, grace, and energy. Although he was thirty years older than Julia, Tyler began courting her.

▲ *Tyler set the stage for Hawaii's statehood.*

Julia Gardiner ▶
Tyler

In June 1844, the couple was secretly married in New York City. Of course, the marriage could not be hidden for very long. When the president and his new bride arrived in Washington, the capital was already buzzing with the news. Tyler was the first president to marry while in office.

Julia Tyler was a charming and popular first lady. She dressed with style and loved to spend money. She threw huge, lively parties in the White House. The president adored his new wife, who was younger than some of his children. Julia wrote to her mother, "Nothing appears to delight the President more than . . . to hear people sing my praises."

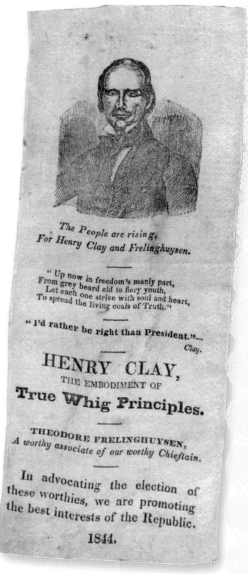

▾ *An 1844 campaign ribbon for Henry Clay*

Julia also started a presidential custom that continues to this day. After she became first lady, she ordered that the song "Hail to the Chief" be played each time Tyler appeared at a special event. The song was based on a poem called "The Lady of the Lake," written in 1810 by Sir Walter Scott.

In 1844, Tyler began thinking about running for reelection. Neither the Whigs nor the Democrats would have him. Instead, the Democrats chose Tennessee politician James K. Polk to run. The Whigs picked Tyler's long-time enemy, Henry Clay.

James K. Polk ▶

Tyler decided to form a third party. He called it the Democratic-Republican Party. Using the slogan "Tyler and Texas," the president rallied support for his cause. It soon became clear, however, that Tyler could not win. He gave up his run and threw his support behind Polk. Like Tyler, Polk was in favor of annexing Texas. This idea was popular with much of the public. It helped carry Polk to victory.

On March 1, 1845, just three days before he left office, Tyler signed a resolution to annex Texas. Nine months after Tyler left office, Texas became the twenty-eighth U.S. state. Tyler considered annexing Texas to be his greatest achievement. He believed that he would be remembered forever for adding Texas to the Union.

◀ *The flag of the Republic of Texas*

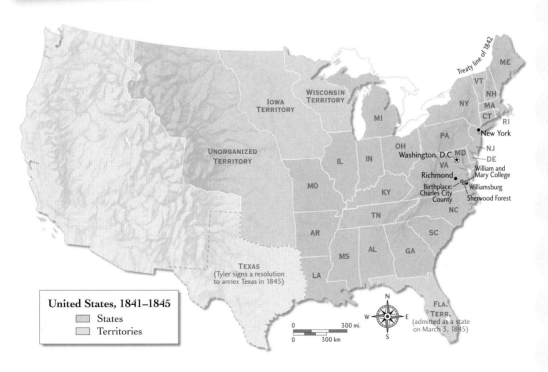

United States, 1841–1845

- States
- Territories

Later Life

★ ★ ★

The Tylers retired to Sherwood Forest, their new plantation in Virginia. Although a New Yorker by birth, Julia
quickly settled into her new role as a Southern lady. She
supported all of her husband's causes. She also accepted
slavery as a fact of life in the South. Over the next few

*The Tylers' Sherwood ▾
Forest plantation
in Virginia*

years, the pair had seven children. In all, Tyler had fifteen living children, the most of any president. His youngest child, Pearl, was born in 1860 when Tyler was seventy years old.

Tyler was quite happy to retire from politics. He spent the next fifteen years at home, managing Sherwood Forest and its seventy slaves. Tyler was out of the spotlight, but he still paid attention to current events.

In 1860, Abraham Lincoln was elected president.

▼ *Abraham Lincoln*

Many Southerners were afraid Lincoln would end slavery. Southern states began to **secede** from the Union. The first state to secede was South Carolina, in December 1860. Mississippi, Florida, Alabama, Georgia, and Louisiana quickly followed. In February, these states joined together to form a new nation called the

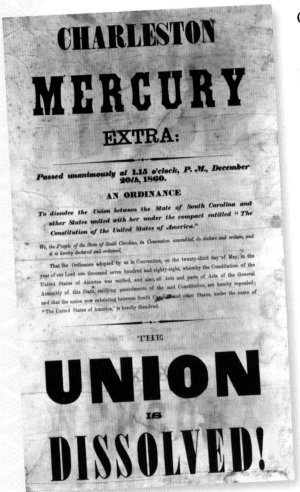

CHARLESTON MERCURY

EXTRA:

Passed unanimously at 1.15 o'clock, P. M., December 20th, 1860.

AN ORDINANCE

To dissolve the Union between the State of South Carolina and other States united with her under the compact entitled "The Constitution of the United States of America."

We, the People of the State of South Carolina, in Convention assembled, do declare and ordain, and it is hereby declared and ordained,

That the Ordinance adopted by us in Convention, on the twenty-third day of May, in the year of our Lord one thousand seven hundred and eighty-eight, whereby the Constitution of the United States of America was ratified, and also, all Acts and parts of Acts of the General Assembly of this State, ratifying amendments of the said Constitution, are hereby repealed; and that the union now subsisting between South Carolina and other States, under the name of "The United States of America," is hereby dissolved.

THE

UNION IS DISSOLVED!

A Southern newspaper announcing the end of the Union

Confederate States of America. Virginia, a border state between the North and the South, was in a difficult spot. The Confederate states wanted Virginia to join them. The United States urged Virginia to stay put. At first, Tyler believed that Virginia should stay in the Union. He hoped that war between the North and the South could be avoided. In a letter to a friend, Tyler wrote, "We have fallen on evil times . . . the day of doom for the great model Republic is at hand."

In February 1861, Tyler agreed to be the chairman at peace talks among the states. He would try to find a way to keep the nation out of war.

The talks were a failure. By the time Tyler returned to Virginia, he was convinced that his state must secede from the United States. In public, Tyler criticized the talks that he had headed. He began making fiery speeches urging Virginia to secede.

In April, Virginia's lawmakers voted to leave the Union and join the Confederate States of America. Virginia placed its armies under the command of Confederate president Jefferson Davis. Although Tyler himself was too old to

◄ *The 1861 inauguration of Jefferson Davis*

fight, several of his sons and grandsons signed up to battle the North.

Tyler wanted to play a part in the growth of his new nation. In November 1861, he was elected to the Confederate Congress. The same month, war between the North and the South began. The Civil War would last four years and cause the deaths of more than five hundred thousand people.

The Battle of ▼
Gettysburg in 1863
was one of the
bloodiest battles
in the Civil War.

Tyler would not live long enough to see bloodshed and destruction rip apart his beloved South. In January, Tyler left Sherwood Forest and traveled to Richmond, Virginia, the Confederate capital. On January 12, 1862, the seventy-one-year-old political leader suffered a stroke. Over the next few days, he seemed to be getting better. Then, on January 18, Tyler took a turn for the worse. His last words were, "Doctor, I am going. . . . Perhaps it is best."

When Tyler died, many people in the nation considered him a traitor to the Union. His death was ignored by President Abraham Lincoln and the rest of Washington's lawmakers.

In the South, however, Tyler was treated as a hero and a patriot. For two days, his coffin lay in the halls of the Confederate Congress. Confederate president Davis and many others paid their respects to Tyler and his family. On January 20, 1862, Tyler's coffin was draped with the Confederate flag and carried to Hollywood

▼ *John Tyler's coffin was covered by the Confederate flag, shown here on the cover of a musical composition dedicated to Jefferson Davis.*

John Tyler's grave in Richmond, Virginia ▲

Cemetery in Richmond. There, the tenth president of the United States was laid to rest next to another president from Virginia, James Monroe.

John Tyler's one term as U.S. president was marked by bitter conflict with Congress. His presidency, however, was important for many reasons. He paved the way for adding Texas and Hawaii to the Union. He also helped promote settlement in the West. Most important, Tyler set the standard for an orderly transfer of power upon the death of a president.

When Tyler died, he was not a U.S. citizen. By joining the Confederacy in 1861, he had given up his citizenship. More than one hundred years later, President Jimmy Carter restored Tyler's citizenship, making him once again a member of the nation that meant so much to him throughout his life.

GLOSSARY

★ ★ ★

cabinet—a president's group of advisers who are the heads of government departments

campaign—the effort to win an election

Constitution—the document stating the basic laws of the United States

effigy—a rough dummy representing a hated person

hard cider—an alcoholic drink

impeach—to charge a public official with a serious crime

paralyzed—unable to move

plantation—a large farm

resolution—a formal statement of an opinion passed by Congress

secede—withdraw from

slogan—a phrase used to capture public attention in a campaign

states' rights—the belief that all powers not given to the federal government in the Constitution belong to the states

stroke—a problem in the brain causing a sudden loss of the ability to feel or move

turncoat—someone who switches to an opposing side

vetoed—refused to approve, which prevented a measure from taking effect

JOHN TYLER'S LIFE AT A GLANCE

★ ★ ★

PERSONAL

Nickname: Accidental President, His Accidency

Born: March 29, 1790, in Charles County, Virginia

Father's name: John Tyler

Mother's name: Mary Armistead Tyler

Education: Graduated from the College of William and Mary in 1807

Wives' names: Letitia Christian Tyler (1790–1842); Julia Gardiner Tyler (1820–1889)

Married: March 29, 1813; June 26, 1844

Children: Mary Tyler (1815–1848); Robert Tyler (1816–1877); John Tyler (1819–1896); Letitia Tyler (1821–1907); Elizabeth Tyler (1823–1850); Anne Contesse Tyler (1825); Alice Tyler (1827–1854); Tazewell Tyler (1830–1874); David Gardiner Tyler (1846–1927); John Alexander Tyler (1848–1883); Julia Gardiner Tyler (1849–1871); Lachlan Tyler (1851–1902); Lyon Gardiner Tyler (1853–1935); Robert Fitzwalter Tyler (1856–1927); Pearl Tyler (1860–1947)

Died: January 18, 1862, in Richmond, Virginia

Buried: Hollywood Cemetery in Richmond, Virginia

John Tyler's
Life at a Glance

PUBLIC

Occupation before presidency:	Lawyer, politician
Occupation after presidency:	Member of the Confederate House of Representatives
Military service:	None
Other government positions:	Member of the Virginia House of Delegates; representative from Virginia in the U.S. House of Representatives; governor of Virginia; U.S. senator from Virginia; vice president
Political party:	Whig
Vice president:	None
Dates in office:	April 6, 1841–March 4, 1845
Presidential opponent:	None
Number of votes (Electoral College):	Not elected
Writings:	None

★

John Tyler's Cabinet

Secretary of state:
Daniel Webster (1841–1843)
Abel P. Upshur (1843–1844)
John C. Calhoun (1844–1845)

Secretary of the treasury:
Thomas Ewing (1841)
Walter Forward (1841–1843)
John C. Spencer (1843–1844)
George M. Bibb (1844–1845)

Secretary of war:
John Bell (1841)
John C. Spencer (1841–1843)
James M. Porter (1843–1844)
William Wilkins (1844–1845)

Attorney general:
John J. Crittenden (1841)
Hugh S. Legare (1841–1843)
John Nelson (1843–1845)

Postmaster general:
Francis Granger (1841)
Charles A. Wickliffe (1841–1845)

Secretary of the navy:
George E. Badger (1841)
Abel P. Upshur (1841–1843)
David Henshaw (1843–1844)
Thomas W. Gilmer (1844)
John Y. Mason (1844–1845)

JOHN TYLER'S LIFE AND TIMES

★ ★ ★

TYLER'S LIFE

WORLD EVENTS

March 29, Tyler is born in Charles City County, Virginia (below)   1790

1790

1791   Austrian composer Wolfgang Amadeus Mozart (above) dies

1792   The dollar currency is introduced to America

1799   Napoléon Bonaparte takes control of France

The Rosetta stone, which was the key to understanding Egyptian hieroglyphics, is found near Rosetta, Egypt

TYLER'S LIFE

WORLD EVENTS

1800

1801   German scientist Johann Ritter discovers ultraviolet radiation

1805   General anesthesia is first used in surgery

Graduates from William and Mary College (above)   1807

1807   Robert Fulton's *Clermont* (above) is the first reliable steamship to travel between New York City and Albany

Begins practicing law in Virginia   1809

1809   American poet and short-story writer Edgar Allen Poe is born in Boston

1810 1810   Bernardo O'Higgins (below) leads Chile in its fight for independence from Spain

Appointed to the Virginia House of Delegates   1811

TYLER'S LIFE

WORLD EVENTS

	1812– 1814 The United States and Great Britain fight the War of 1812 (below)

March 29, marries   **1813**
Letitia Christian
(left)

1814– 1815   European states meet in Vienna, Austria, to redraw national borders after the conclusion of the Napoleonic Wars

Serves in the   **1817-**
U.S. House of   **1821**
Representatives

1820   1820   Susan B. Anthony (right), a leader of the American woman suffrage movement, is born

1821   Central American countries gain independence from Spain

1823   Mexico becomes a republic

Elected governor   **1825**
of Virginia

1826   The first photograph is taken by Joseph Niépce, a French physicist

TYLER'S LIFE

Serves in the U.S. Senate	1827-1840

Elected vice president under William Henry Harrison — 1840

April 4, President Harrison dies — 1841

April 6, Tyler is sworn in as president

Vetoes a bill for a new Bank of the United States

Vetoes a second national bank bill; all but one member of Tyler's cabinet quits in protest

Thrown out of the Whig Party

WORLD EVENTS

1827 Modern-day matches are invented by coating the end of a wooden stick with phosphorus

1829 The first practical sewing machine (right) is invented by French tailor Barthélemy Thimonnier

1830

1833 Great Britain abolishes slavery

1836 Texans defeat Mexican troops at San Jacinto after a deadly battle at the Alamo (right)

1840

1840 Auguste Rodin, famous sculptor of *The Thinker* (below), is born

TYLER'S LIFE

WORLD EVENTS

Ends the war against
the Seminole Indians

1842

September 10,
Letitia Tyler dies

1843 American industrialist
and philanthropist
Cornelius Vanderbilt
is born in Staten
Island, New York

The United States
begins trading
with China for
the first time

1844

June 26, marries Julia
Gardiner, becoming
the first president to
get married in office

March 1,
the United
States signs a
resolution to
annex Texas

1845

March 3, Florida is
admitted into the
United States

1848 *The Communist
Manifesto,* by German
writer Karl Marx
(above), is widely
distributed

TYLER'S LIFE

WORLD EVENTS

1850

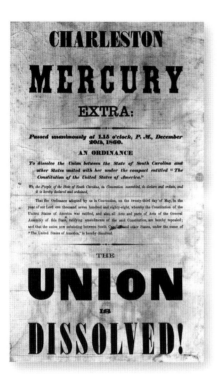

1852   American Harriet Beecher Stowe (right) publishes *Uncle Tom's Cabin*

1858   English scientist Charles Darwin (right) presents his theory of evolution

1860

1860   Austrian composer Gustav Mahler is born in Kalischt (now in Austria)

February, heads a   **1861**
Southern attempt to
work out a settlement
to avoid the Civil War

November, is
elected to the Con-
federate Congress

January 18, dies in   **1862**
Richmond, Virginia

UNDERSTANDING JOHN TYLER AND HIS PRESIDENCY

★ ★ ★

IN THE LIBRARY

Ferry, Steven. *John Tyler: Our 10th President.*
Chanhassen, Minn.: The Child's World, 2001.

Lillegard, Dee. *John Tyler: Tenth President of the United States.*
Chicago: Childrens Press, 1987.

O'Connell, Kim A. *John Tyler.*
Springfield, N.J.: Enslow, 2002.

Welsbacher, Anne. *John Tyler.*
Minneapolis: Abdo Publishers, 2000.

ON THE WEB

For more information on this topic, use FactHound.

1. Go to *www.facthound.com*
2. Type in this book ID: 0756502586
3. Click on the *Fetch It* button.

FactHound will find the best Web sites for you.

TYLER HISTORIC SITES
ACROSS THE COUNTRY

Hollywood Cemetery
412 South Cherry Street
Richmond, VA 23220
804/648-8501
To visit Tyler's grave

Sherwood Forest Plantation
14501 John Tyler Highway
Charles City, VA 23030
804/829-5377
To visit Tyler's home from 1842
until his death in 1862

THE U.S. PRESIDENTS
(Years in Office)

★ ★ ★

1. **George Washington**
   (March 4, 1789-March 3, 1797)
2. **John Adams**
   (March 4, 1797-March 3, 1801)
3. **Thomas Jefferson**
   (March 4, 1801-March 3, 1809)
4. **James Madison**
   (March 4, 1809-March 3, 1817)
5. **James Monroe**
   (March 4, 1817-March 3, 1825)
6. **John Quincy Adams**
   (March 4, 1825-March 3, 1829)
7. **Andrew Jackson**
   (March 4, 1829-March 3, 1837)
8. **Martin Van Buren**
   (March 4, 1837-March 3, 1841)
9. **William Henry Harrison**
   (March 6, 1841-April 4, 1841)
10. **John Tyler**
    (April 6, 1841-March 3, 1845)
11. **James K. Polk**
    (March 4, 1845-March 3, 1849)
12. **Zachary Taylor**
    (March 5, 1849-July 9, 1850)
13. **Millard Fillmore**
    (July 10, 1850-March 3, 1853)
14. **Franklin Pierce**
    (March 4, 1853-March 3, 1857)
15. **James Buchanan**
    (March 4, 1857-March 3, 1861)
16. **Abraham Lincoln**
    (March 4, 1861-April 15, 1865)
17. **Andrew Johnson**
    (April 15, 1865-March 3, 1869)

18. **Ulysses S. Grant**
    (March 4, 1869-March 3, 1877)
19. **Rutherford B. Hayes**
    (March 4, 1877-March 3, 1881)
20. **James Garfield**
    (March 4, 1881-Sept 19, 1881)
21. **Chester Arthur**
    (Sept 20, 1881-March 3, 1885)
22. **Grover Cleveland**
    (March 4, 1885-March 3, 1889)
23. **Benjamin Harrison**
    (March 4, 1889-March 3, 1893)
24. **Grover Cleveland**
    (March 4, 1893-March 3, 1897)
25. **William McKinley**
    (March 4, 1897-
    September 14, 1901)
26. **Theodore Roosevelt**
    (September 14, 1901-
    March 3, 1909)
27. **William Howard Taft**
    (March 4, 1909-March 3, 1913)
28. **Woodrow Wilson**
    (March 4, 1913-March 3, 1921)
29. **Warren G. Harding**
    (March 4, 1921-August 2, 1923)
30. **Calvin Coolidge**
    (August 3, 1923-March 3, 1929)
31. **Herbert Hoover**
    (March 4, 1929-March 3, 1933)
32. **Franklin D. Roosevelt**
    (March 4, 1933-April 12, 1945)

33. **Harry S. Truman**
    (April 12, 1945-
    January 20, 1953)
34. **Dwight D. Eisenhower**
    (January 20, 1953-
    January 20, 1961)
35. **John F. Kennedy**
    (January 20, 1961-
    November 22, 1963)
36. **Lyndon B. Johnson**
    (November 22, 1963-
    January 20, 1969)
37. **Richard M. Nixon**
    (January 20, 1969-
    August 9, 1974)
38. **Gerald R. Ford**
    (August 9, 1974-
    January 20, 1977)
39. **James Earl Carter**
    (January 20, 1977-
    January 20, 1981)
40. **Ronald Reagan**
    (January 20, 1981-
    January 20, 1989)
41. **George H. W. Bush**
    (January 20, 1989-
    January 20, 1993)
42. **William Jefferson Clinton**
    (January 20, 1993-
    January 20, 2001)
43. **George W. Bush**
    (January 20, 2001-)